Icons

Jonathan Reeve Price

Copyright

Computer images reviewed in this book come from Apple Inc., Microsoft, Inc., and the Material Design standards of Alphabet, Inc.
The images of Catharina of Alexandria, and the Evangelist, come from the Rijksmuseum, Amsterdam, the Netherlands.

.

Publisher::
The Communication Circle
4704 Mi Cordelia Drive, NW
Albuquerque, NM 87120
Published in the United States of America

First Publication: 2024
ISBN-10: 0-9719954-8-6
ISBN-13: 978-0-9719954-8-2

For Lisa

Contents

Introduction

An icon is an image that has mysterious powers. In a church, the devout kneel in front of the statue or painting of a saint, light candles, and pray to the divine being represented in the icon, asking that spirit to act on their behalf. Through the icon we interact with the invisible.

On a computer, an icon is more practical. Take this picture of a printer.

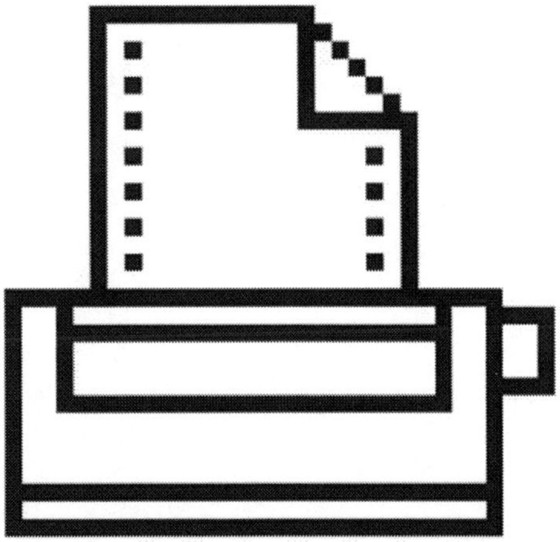

We have all seen a lot of printers. Most do not look like this. But we have learned that this image, based on some long-ago model of a printer, stands for whatever printer we have access to. This image is an abstract representation of a physical object.

But it has agency. This icon offers to do something for us—at a distance.

We cannot write or even read the hundreds of lines of code that bring up the Print dialog and wake up the printer. But we have learned that the icon can do all this for us. So we give it a tap.

And the icon responds.

Immediately, we see a change in the shading of the icon—reassuring us that, yes, we did succeed in triggering the icon—and, then, overlaying the window, we see a dialog appear. This instant feedback makes it seem as if the icon itself is doing something, acting on our behalf.

Like a door handle allowing us to open a door, the icon indicates where we can act, and suggests what that benefit that action will afford us. And, if we engage with it, the icon issues a command to the unseen elements deep inside the computer. The icon does not actually do the work. Code does. But to appeal to the invisible code we interact through the computer icon.

These little gizmos have been around for more than fifty years. They're innocuous, almost unnoticed elements within the complex visual displays on our phones, tablets, or computer screens. Such small, simple drawings are made up of individual dots or squares arranged in a grid, without any shading, color, or subtlety. When we really look at one of these images, enlarged, we see an austere aesthetic, a stripped-down, miniaturized gestalt that hints at, and hides its underlying power.

But behind each icon, I hear people—graphic artists coming up with the shapes, programmers preparing the code that our tap will activate, designers fitting these shapes into a full user interface, other users struggling to understand what the icons might do, cultural historians pondering the historical artifacts that are embedded in these images, and, behind any particular application, I hear the giants—Apple and Google, for example—generating thousands of these little pictures to stand for every function that code may offer within their ecosystems.

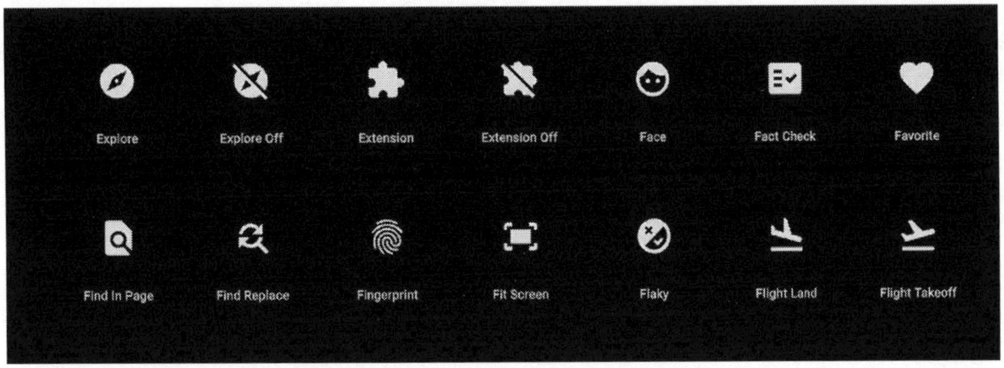

To me, icons act as small poems, austere artworks, tiny programs. As I hold each one up to the light, I enlarge the image to study it as a visual object, I reflect on its label, I wonder about its true function, I hear, in the background, the arguments and attitudes of the developers, and, around me in the ether, I sense the complaints of other "users." I explore, I listen, I suffer. And I remember.

When I went to work for Apple Computer on May Day 1982, there were no icons. As a technical communicator, I wrote on a personal computer called the Apple III. Its screen showed 24 lines of green letters on a black background, with a maximum of 80 characters per line. The interface was text.

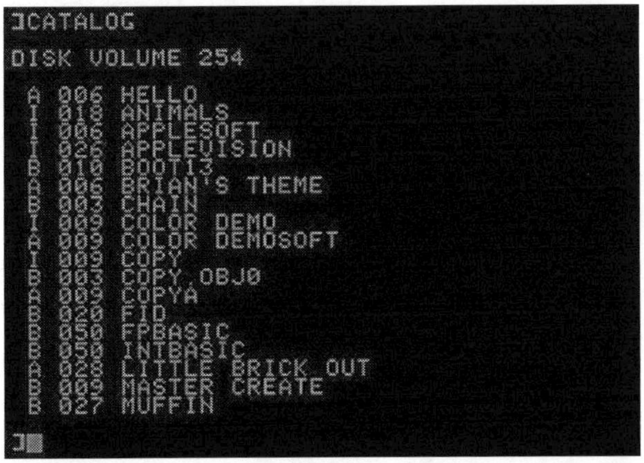

Think of it. To tell the printer to emphasize a word, I had to tap an arrow key to move the cursor just to the left of the word, then type a code such as <b> to boldface the word, then, using the right arrow key, I had to move the cursor to the end of the word, and type another code, such as </b>, to turn off boldfacing.

<b>important</b>

Software told the printer what to do with these codes, as it slapped my content onto green-and-white computer paper.

But at the same time, in another building on Bandley Drive, under a pirate flag, Steve Jobs was creating the Macintosh, with a screen that showed what your printout would actually look like. (The marketing folks called this "What You See is What You Get"). What a delight when I finally got my own pre-production Mac!

A device called a mouse drove a pointer on the screen, so I could intervene directly with the text on the screen. I no longer had to type any commands. Instead, commands appeared in a list on screen—a menu.

With a mouse, I could now click the word Print in that menu, and the document would zip off to the printer.

The real miracle was MacPaint. I could now draw on the computer. No longer was the screen a bunch of rows and columns with letters or numbers. Moving my mouse I could make swirls, curls, dots, and shapes right on the screen, like this picture by the designer Susan Kare.

Because the computer was built from the board up as a graphic machine, Andy Hertzfeld, one of the star programmers, hired Susan Kare to duplicate some commands, such as Print, as images. Placing tiny black squares into a very small grid, she built up a picture you could click.

To save a file on that first Mac, you clicked an image of a floppy disk.

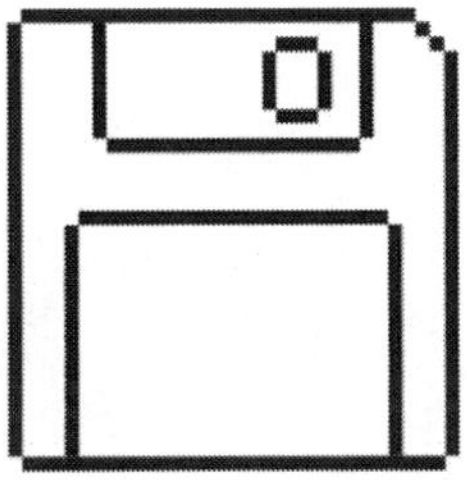

To get rid of a file, you move it over an image of a trash can.

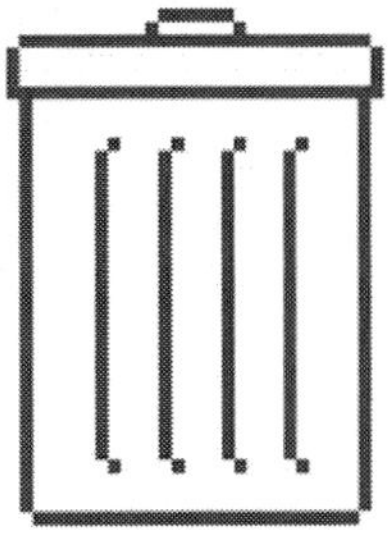

My job was to tell beginning users how to take advantage of this new thing, the graphic interface. But what should we call these active little pictures?

I talked with programmers, designers, marketing folks, and other writers, debating terms. Should these things be called *agents*—because they could receive input, and, somehow, send off a command? Or were they *symbols*, because they stood for, or represented metaphorically, actions and objects?

Eventually we all agreed to call them "icons." The word *Icon* is a kind of geek poetry. The term carries multiple overtones that work together to identify—and glorify—this odd thingamajig.

One of the overtones is religious. In a church or temple, an icon such as a statue of a saint or a painting of a divine being may offer us a visible representation of a spirit we cannot see with our physical eyes.

Interacting with the icon through prayer or offerings, we hope, may persuade that spiritual being to act on our behalf. In this way, an icon offers a miracle.

And it is art. In renaissance paintings, we often see a dozen objects laid out on a table, or draped over a monarch's shoulders…objects related to mythological or Biblical stories, suggesting the powers and virtues of the person in the painting.

Such trappings require interpretation, so that we can understand the moral argument, and see through the apparent to the spirituality underneath. Beauty beckons us to imagine what this king or queen does for the realm, even if we cannot see how that might happen.

Another overtone is semantic. The icon is an arbitrary sign; it lives on conventions that tell us that, somehow, it stands for an object, and it refers to an action involving that object. Taken as a set, icons form a system, a made-up combination of recurrent signs, like an artificial language, full of connotations that extend meaning way beyond whatever the picture itself may denote. So these new symbols, the icons, echoed ideas then current in linguistics and semiology.

But what did these signs mean?

When I watched people using our early software, I realized that, no matter how good Susan Kare's drawings were, many people had trouble understanding what they represented.

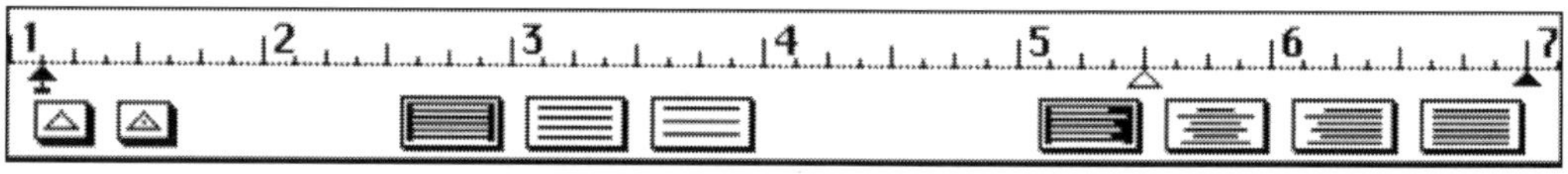

Yes, a few brave people just clicked an unfamiliar icon to find out what it would do. But most people ignored all the icons until they needed to do something specific as part of their work on a document, say, or a spreadsheet. The work context led them to expect that certain functions should be available.

But how? Where?

Some people articulated their goal to themselves in words such as *Add*, or *Total*, while other people envisioned pictures of the object or action, like paper emerging from an adding machine. With those words or images in mind, they pondered the list of commands in the menu, and scanned the row or box full of icons hoping to find something that more or less mapped to that goal.

Does any menu item represent the action I want to do? Or is there an icon that represents an object, like an adding machine?

But for many users, our icons remained enigmatic, inert, unexpressive.

So as a team, we writers began to argue that the programmers ought to add a label underneath each icon—naming it, or saying what it would do for you.

Our boss, Steve Jobs, hated the very idea. His machine was a graphic marvel, and if we added labels to images, that might ruin their purity. Labels would be a compromise, a concession to pedestrian thinking, a violation of beauty.

Eventually, when Steve was out of the loop, we added a text label underneath each icon. But quite often the text chunk took up vital space, and, worse, it compromised the visual elegance of simple images floating in space.

Hiding and revealing some labels, as needed, offered a partial solution. If you hovered over an icon, its name would appear, briefly, below it. When you moved the cursor away, the label would disappear. Without intruding on the design of the page, the attached label made the icon's meaning more explicit.

But even with that label, our testing showed people struggling with the icons on the screen. These images were so small that people manipulating the pointer with the mouse found them too hard to click.

Engineers decided to enlarge the target area by creating an invisible circle or rectangle around the icon. When a pointer came near enough to click the icon, the area came awake with grey, indicating, yes, you can click anywhere in this area. But now we needed a second image of the icon, to stand out amid the highlighting.

And because the icon had become a button, it had to respond. Soon designers were creating several versions of each icon: one version of the icon showed that it was ready to be used, another showed that you had entered the clickable area, and a third showed yes, you have successfully clicked the icon, issuing its command. As the user acted, then, the underlying code fetched the different versions of the image as feedback. Today, fifty years later, we take these transformations for granted. But back then, the icon seemed to be taking on multitudinous life.

Over time, Apple developed standard sets of icons for use by anyone developing software for the Mac, the iPhone, the iPad. Google matched that with more than three thousand icons in their Material Design collection. You can now download these standardized icons in several different file formats, hues, sizes, weights, and fills. Companies now mix visible labels with hovertext, as in Microsoft Word.

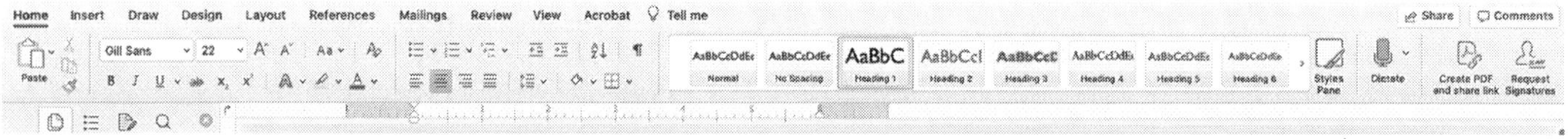

And most companies that create their own software now develop extensive guidelines for using these icons in their user interface…when to use them, where, which ones, what kind of labels to use, what code to apply, how to report problems. These styleguides can run into hundreds of pages.

On your screen, you'll notice even more metaphors, such as the colored icons representing apps--tap to launch--and labels that look like icons, but perform no action. Onscreen we live in a forest of symbols, ranging from glyphs (symbols in a line of text) to dancing circles and status bars. We have become fluent in emojis, and we create our own avatars.

These metaphors, these visual signs, are a tribute to the invention of the graphic user interface half a century ago…but they will all be giving away to the new interface, where instead of tapping, speaking, or typing to issue a command, we describe the end result we desire, and let a more powerful intelligence act on our behalf.

We have come a long way from those one-story buildings back on Bandley Drive, where roosters visited from the farm next door.

In this book, I interrogate a hundred icons from the 3,000 now available as part of Google's Material Design set.

I ponder questions such as:

- Is the image beautiful?
- Does the shape invite me to tap?
- Does the picture telegraph what the icon can do for me?
- What exactly is its function?
- What does the name, or label, suggest?
- Does the icon seem to take an attitude —toward me, toward other users?
- What are the overtones, the vibrations, I pick up?
- Does the icon retain some mysterious power?

We've used many of these icons so often that they seem natural, routine, hardly worth thinking about. Good. That's the way they are supposed to be used.

But if we pause to listen, I believe that we can hear a distant music.

360

To circle around an object

Imagination cannot show me such a tour.
This icon launches code,
Spins the Earth around its axis,
Turns a city street into a whirl,
And races like an angel around a volcano.
Going nowhere fast, the blur
Amazes eyes, and numbs
My hypnotized intelligence.

attachment

To send a file with your email

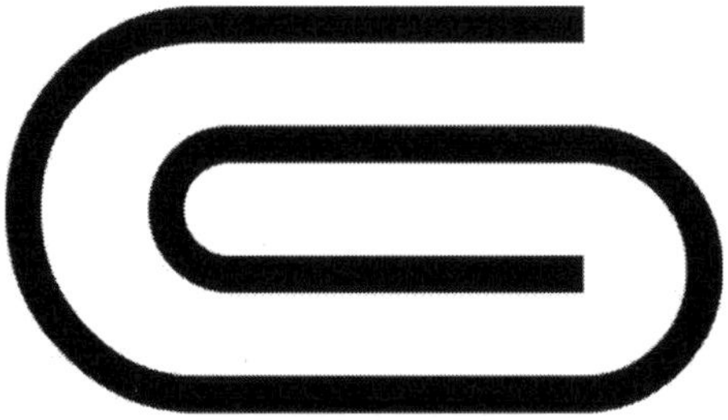

How hard it is to give up what we love,
Abandoning nostalgia, swimming past
Sentiment! With one click, we make
The past into an icon, like
This old metal paperclip, reminder
Of paper pages, contracts to be signed.
Today my heart still makes the tie, and ego
Runs around the track to find and open
Each precious image, each self-important file.

brush

To set the tip, stroke, opacity,
color, or flow as you paint

This ancient tool says take me in your hand,
Feel the soft bristles, dip them, and paint.
But its icon makes us go virtually
From the physical into a pixel path.
All we lose is the smell, the dirty rag, and life.

email

To create a message that you can send over the internet

Who uses envelopes today?
The flap, the licked glue,
The stamp--how quaint!
With each tap of this icon, we let
The physical go, bending toward
An electronic doppelganger.

favorite

To show you like something
or someone

How many meanings this sign enacts.
It performs as noun, verb, and glyph,
Bumper sticker, t-shirt, cheap gift.
In interface, a momentary fling,
It acts to save, or store, its image
Pointed, yes, but always curving
From a delicate nub into a full heart.

gesture

To draw freehand

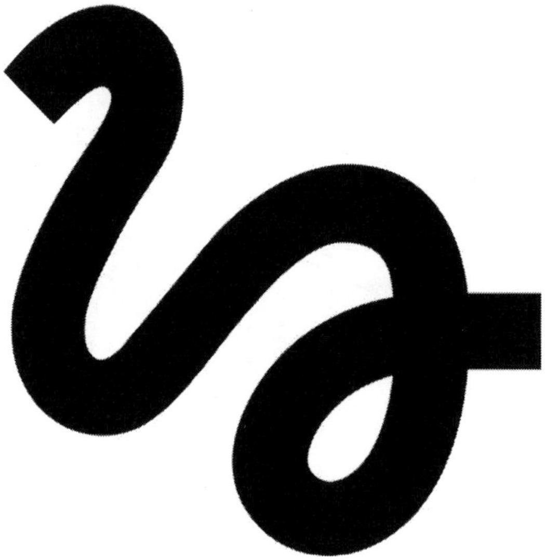

How imprecise touch can be, but how direct!
Squiggling, tapping, pinching or panning,
We drag an element into view, or out, swiping
Beyond a sensitive threshold to complete the act.
Like a snake approaching Eve in paradise
This teasing icon invites the finger-tip.

grid_on

To mark the drawing surface
with squares

How much a grid can say
When each object gets its spot!
We can see how each relates
To neighbor, hierarchy, and frame.
So imagination ranges across
The whole, allowing
Meaning to arise from symmetry.

image

To add a picture
to your post

Why two pyramids, or are these
Mountain peaks? How can such an
Icon stand for every image?
Perhaps this shorthand for imagination includes
The black we see when we close our eyes,
Tiny stars, and the unknown we share within.

radar

To track weather moving
across the map

As we muse, we scan the full 360,
Sending out waves we cannot see,
Receiving back faint signals, blips, and
An occasional flash to absorb.
Perhaps when we turn on this radar
We contemplate our own geography.

power

To turn the device on or off

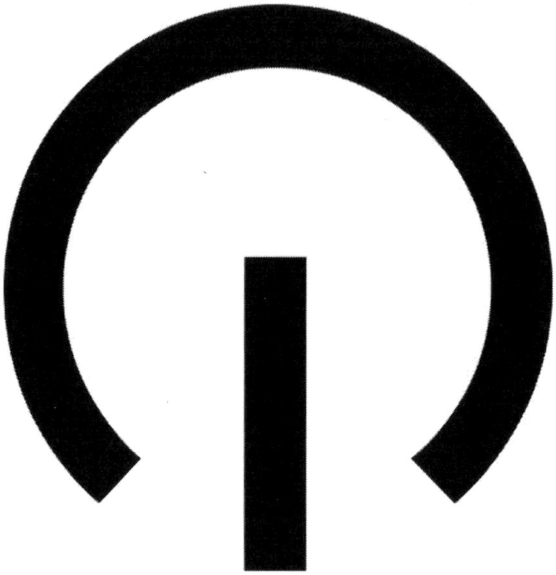

How delicate the enfolding curves, the high nub
Waiting to be turned on, or off, the switch attuned
To touch, balanced between aware and numb, begging
For us to click, tap, rub, or push, just once to start,
And again, once, to make the energy fade to null.

home

To go back to the landing page,
or starting point, on a site

Caught in the architecture of an indeterminate space
We yearn to climb to the roof, to escape,
Fast, from the maze of corridors and stairwells
In and down and back and around.
This icon draws us back to the one house
Where Mom still opens the front door.

price_tag

To display the hidden price

My name's a tag, but the amount is blank.
I claim to set the price, but markets interfere--
Markdowns, discounts, sales, and bankruptcy
Erase my value, and black out my economy.

account_balance

To find out how much you own—or owe

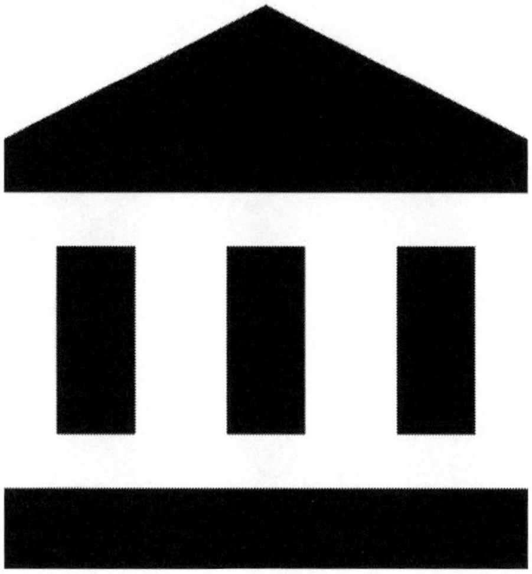

Nothing says bank like a Greek temple
Holding your money, blocking
You from whatever is left, after
Accounting for interest, theft, and fees—
How do we weigh this image, gauge
The actual columns of loss?

add_card

To expand your virtual wallet

Turning the plastic into code, we can expand
Our artificial wallet, ready to tap. Almost
Inaudible, this new account approves,
Recalculates, and tracks whatever, where, and when
We buy. But hovering is not paying, we imagine,
And convenience masks the debt.

currency_exchange

To learn what your money is worth
in another currency

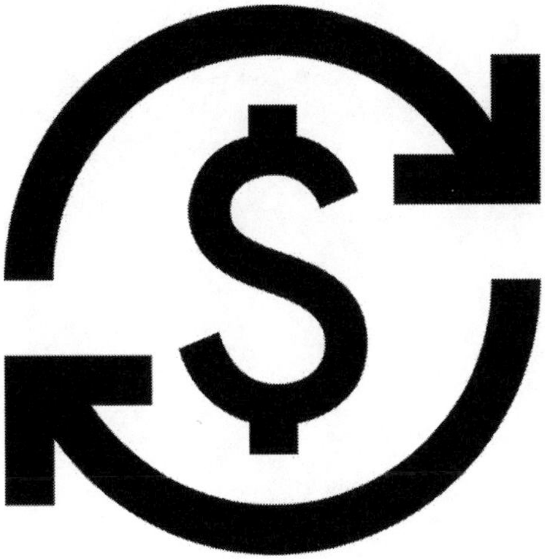

An economy in miniature, it senses
The velocity of one dollar spinning
Through every trade and currency,
Obliterating trace, laundering
And cashing out,
Circling the cost of change.

contactless_pay

To pick up the signal
from your credit card

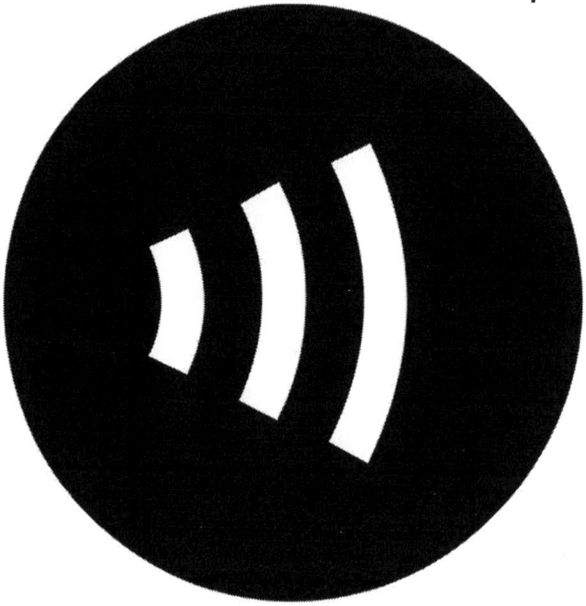

In the near field, we can evade
Kooties, germs, viruses, and dirt--
But this icon seems to growl.
Perhaps,like us, it misses human touch.

shopping_cart

To see--and buy--what you've picked

Is this the archetype of America, the bin
We can never fill? We tell ourselves,
Abandon your cart, block
The wheels, and let the ice cream melt.
But, automatons, our fingers tap, submit, and pay.

add_chart

To show selected numbers as shapes

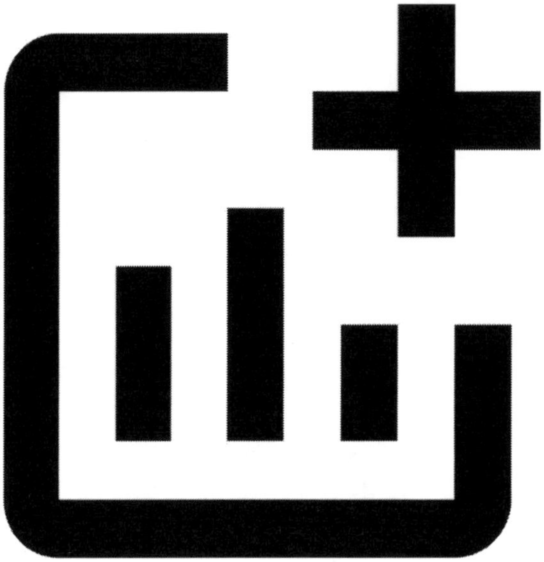

Turn array into flow
Make points scatter
Envision, pivot, and recalculate
Compare and imagine
As if

bubble_chart

To show data points in an x & y grid,
with circles to suggest the sizes (z)

Who makes a map of bubbles, or
Traps circles within a grid? Who
Plots x against y, then inflates the balloon to z?
Determined to break free, we soar
Out of the box, and beyond all formula.

pie_chart

To show how a total amount is divided into categories

What the mind cannot add up, the eye
Sees whole. Where fractions leave us numb,
The slices tempt the mouth to salivate.
Perhaps math can never calculate what
Metaphor lets intuition grasp.

pivot

To flip selected rows and columns
to make a new table

There, that makes it clear, right?
What was a column becomes a bunch of rows
And the rows turn into columns, bang!
I never understood why, or how, and still don't--
Even with this icon trying hard,
I just can't make the turn.

cell_merge

To combine the contents
of neighboring cells

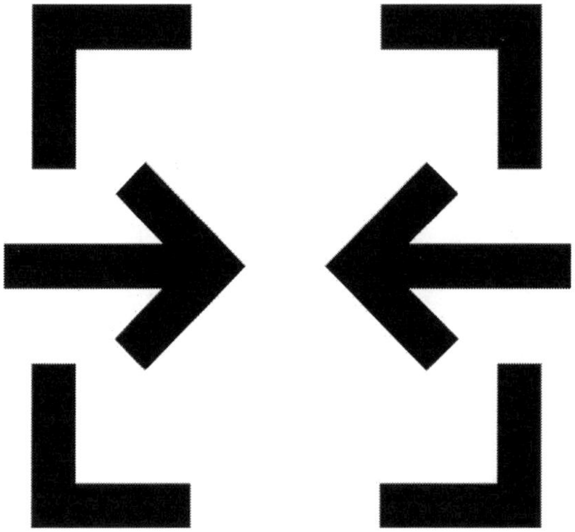

How happy these two cells are to merge, blending
Beyond their rows and columns to metabolize
What they take in, grow, perform, and communicate
Within the full array, becoming more aware, as if
The whole spreadsheet were alive, always wondering,
What if?

insights

To display a dashboard with real-time data, metrics, trends, and forecasts

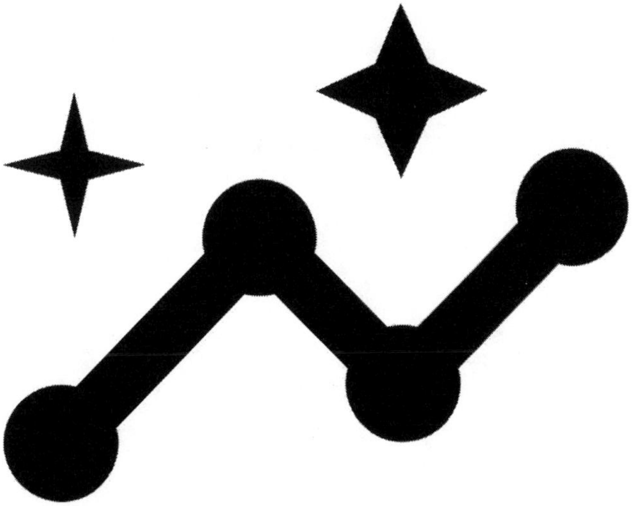

When you look within, is this
What realization brings? Has wisdom
Hit so hard that you see stars?
Enlightenment comes cheap when an icon
Promises to turn numbers into second sight.

database

To show where you'll put data
in a new system

Imagine data pouring like oil
Into a gigantic barrel, inside
A drive as big as a washing machine--
In their stack, these disks used to spin, store
And disgorge tables, keys, and calcs.
Who now can hear that hum?

data_threshold

To set a limit on the values you analyze

Set the sill, then step through the door,
Enter the realm of truth, leave
Out those bad data, like trolls, yelling below,
Inaccurate, incomplete, and dangerous.

dynamic_form

To hide or show fields based on who is using the form, or what they have entered so far

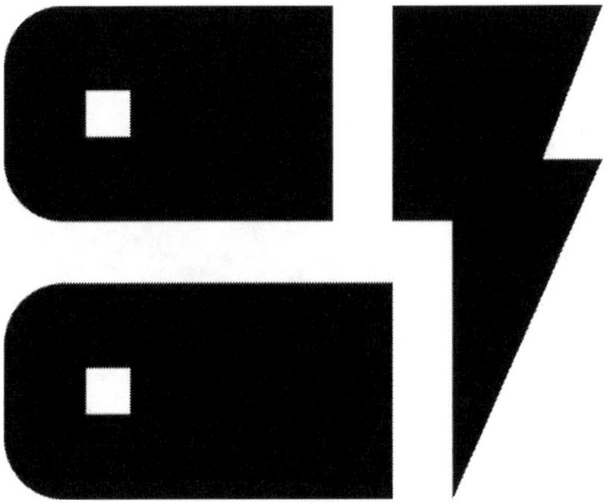

What we show depends on who you are,
What we hide, well, that's conditional.
How valid is your date? How good
Your credit card and fake ID?
For every field you fill, the form
Reconsiders who you are.

join_full

To combine all the rows
in two tables

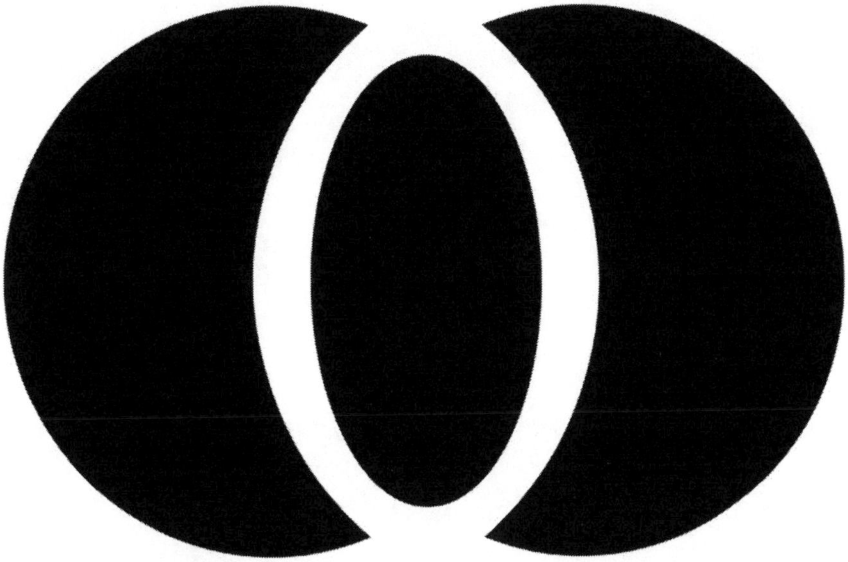

When two black wholes collide,
Zero appears. When two arrays
Become one, all overlap dissolves.
What they had in common, and what was not,
Merge, overwhelming the beauty of Venn.

format_list_bulletted

To turn paragraphs into items in an unnumbered list

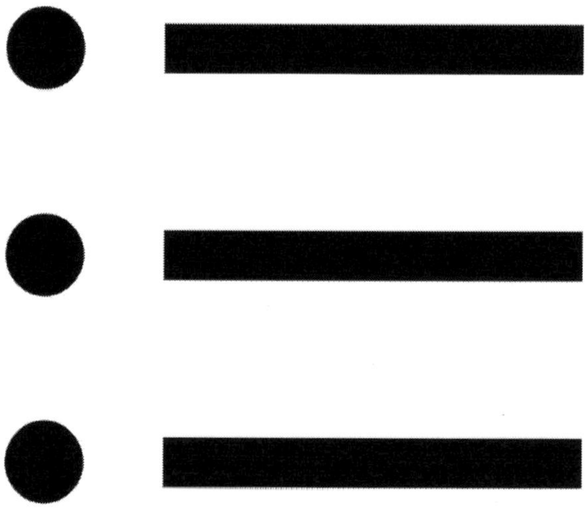

Love 'em or hate 'em, bullets
Separate and show that items form a set.
They insert open space, and give us
White moments before they
Machine gun another point.
Meaning comes in chunks, not flow.

align_horizontal_center

To gather things around an imaginary plumb line

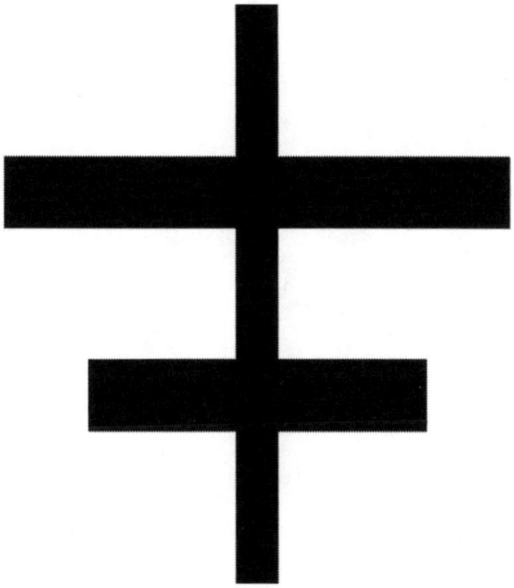

Is this the cross of Lorraine, imposing
Balance and focus on the flow
And sinuous meander of ordinary prose?
Or is this a marker on its grave? Unapologetic,
The icon offers full justification.

settings_brightness

To adjust the amount of light radiating from the screen

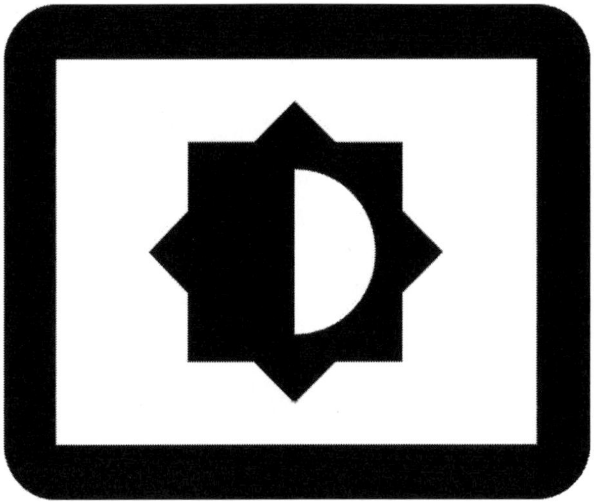

Immerse our eyes in glare, then slide
To dim; imagine we control the sun itself,
Stare into the source, and slowly
Calibrate the waves, making bright bits go
Chiaroscuro, and our own values shade to black.

picture_in_picture

To float one window
on top of others

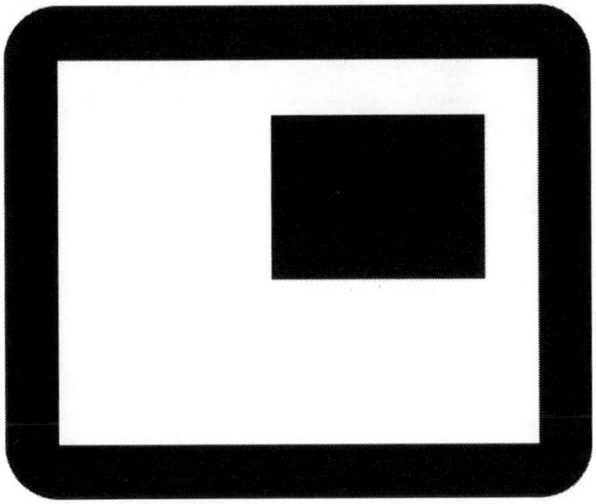

One image contains the echoes of experience,
Evokes, recalls, arouses more than one idea,
Functions like a madeleine, affording
Impulse, drive, and act. And now, with two,
We can encapsulate and multiply,
Making this frame buzz, and my brain blur.

record

To capture sound
or video

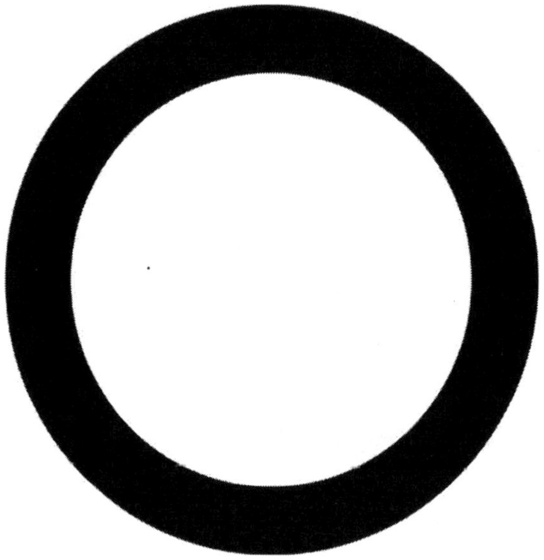

Danger, it says and zero,
An open mouth, about
To say "ah," or "oh,"--
We don't know why, but
We hesitate before we tap.

play

To start audio or video

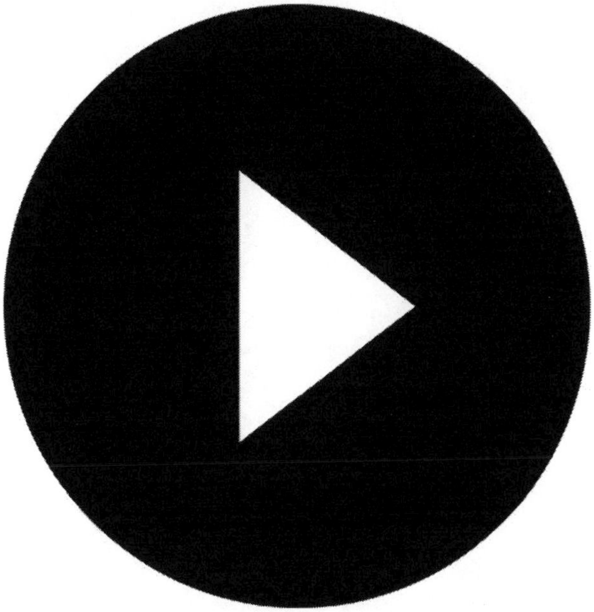

Not fun, or even casual, this button
Points ahead, launches its playback from
The pause or start, and unspools whatever
We have caught or streamed--just tap!
Such sharp light breaks through the dark eye.

noise_aware

To adjust the decibel levels
of your sensors

Attention spreads out into the atmosphere.
Like an open window letting in the soot and sound,
Tuned to whatever arrives, like John Cage
Welcoming air brakes, booms, bursts, and cries,
It widens the circumference of the single soul.

eject

To warn the system that you are
about to unplug a device

Like a sailboat at sunset, or
A pyramid levitated above the Nile,
Out it goes, yanked loose, the plug
Dangling, the image of the device
Erased, all traces of this peripheral
Ghosting the stack, even memory outsourced.

eject_alt

To warn the system that you are about to unplug a device

Is this a cassette
Popping up and out? No--
One tap releases the external drive
So you can yank it loose.
What was a button
Has been reborn as code.

refresh

To bring in new data,
or revive the old

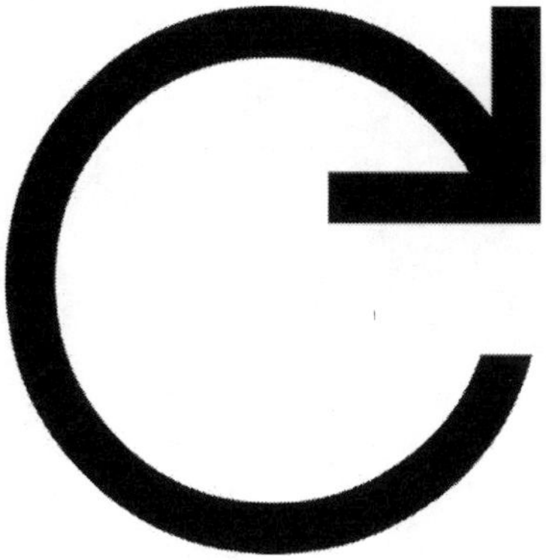

When gibberish appears, or the cursor
Freezes, and I yearn for a magic slate,
I click to go back, following
The endless circumference--
Unlooping the bug, bypassing the crash,
Yes, it says, you can start over,
fresh as a spring day.

track_changes

To show every edit you make

Preserve the ghost of what I cut,
Insert, strike through, remove and--
In comments on the side--
Explain my maze of overlapping lines,
Before I circle back, unpack my editorial mistakes,
And accept, or reject,
Ah, a hundred second thoughts.

search_off

To prevent the browser
from running searches

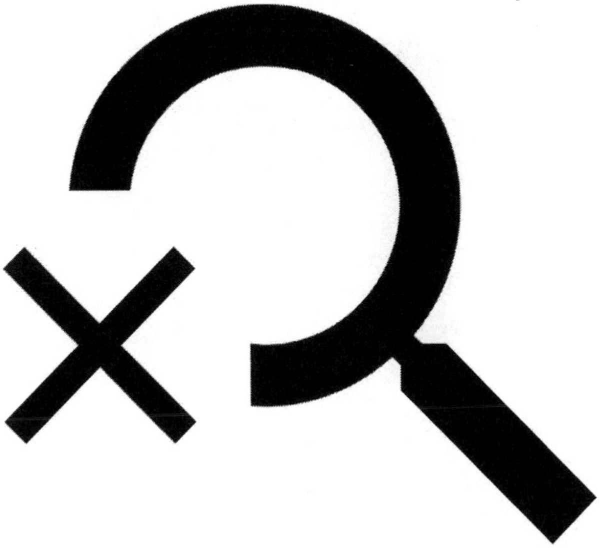

Break the magnifying glass, mark X
On my identity, baffle robots, blank out
My history, and escape the bloodhounds.
Every search attracts an infinity of ads.
I'd rather live within a broken zero.

restore_from_trash

To salvage something
you threw away

I lift the lid, and out comes a raccoon,
Fast, dragging a pizza box, and stained printout.
One click pulls out a body of work, plus
Ten bad drafts, and an unintended download.
Like a movie run in reverse,
This rapture rebuilds the flesh,
And makes my errors live.

memory_chip

To read and write the current program and its data

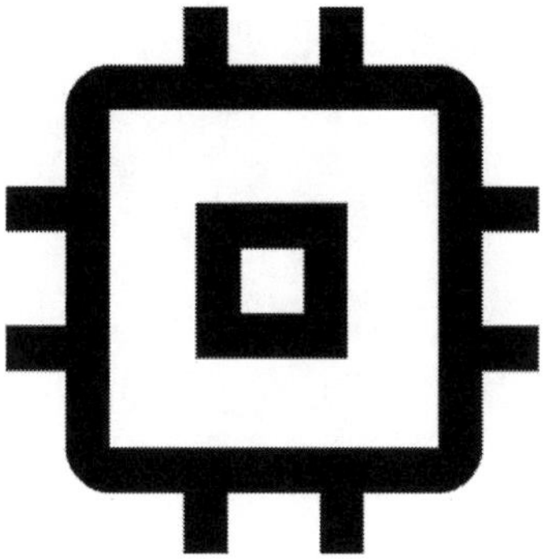

Our brains work faster and more fluidly
Than this chip, where
Memory accumulates in lattices,
And tiny gates shunt ideas as bits,
Implanting thoughts in silicon.
For us, not math but mood
Guides our ship
As we realize and then sail on.

manage_history

To say how many visits, edits, or acts
a program should remember

These gears turn hours around, but years
Grind up the choices I once made. Memory
Edits, imagination rewinds, and this machine
Like karma filters what comes back to life.

change_history

To track each edit you've made

To record, to unearth, to go back--
The three promises of history
Flow backward--they let us erase
The nightmare of mistakes we made,
And transform error into neat geometry.

edit_off

To prevent any change t
format or conter

At one quick click, this icon
Slices through our stubby pencil,
And sends the eraser off into space;
Like a spoiled child,
The owner blocks his ears,
But I hear a malevolent willfulness
Masquerade as Save.

clock_loader

To show time passing
while you open a file

How long will it take for the file to load,
How slow does the network ping?
Software has no room for angst, but
Impatience lives in the finger that taps too fast.
Time's just a slice,
Yearning for the whole pie.

backup

To store a copy of your work

Into the cloud it goes, offloading
The half done, the final, the draft--
Where now does my thought live?
Have all my pixels
Become dust in the overcast,
Pointing to rain?

push_pin

To bring up info about a location

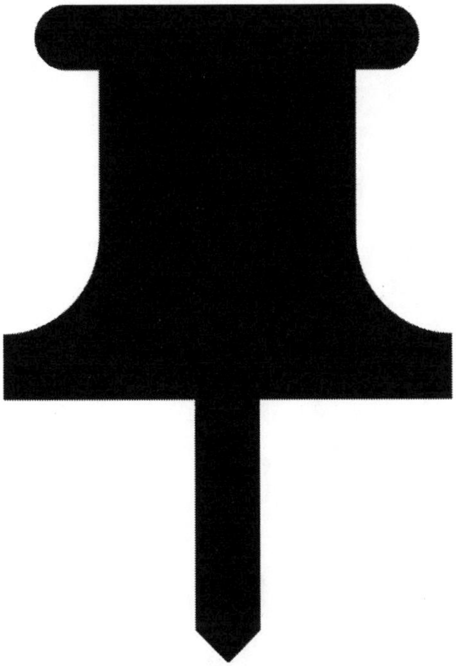

Ouch! The point sticks in
the memory, skewers
meaning into map,

sharp enough to fix
significance, making
coordinating the whole

border_none

To avoid putting a box
around your content

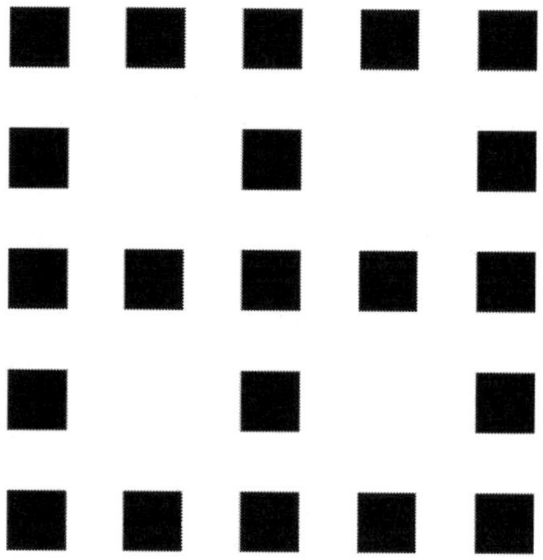

At first, the bounding boxes
Dance and melt, but then
They break apart the boundary,
Free the paragraph,
And let my cell glow
Unboxed.

format_overline

To show that you have
left out letters

How simple and ancient this device,
Putting a line over a letter,
Meaning we have omitted characters.
The icon signals that we have left out
Values that could repeat ad infinitum–
A line decorating eternity.

line_style

To turn a straight line into
dashes or square dots

In art the hand gives feeling to the line,
But here the code itself supplies the bits, hinting
At who I am, and what I want to say--
Ah, Personality without the trace of a brush.

format_paragraph

To end and apply a style
to a paragraph

¶

When did we first need to separate
One idea from the next, leaving a gap
Where the next scribe could put a red mark--
Unlike any character, not a letter, just a sign?
Those blanks at the turn of the lines soon
Said enough, and this unnecessary glyph slid
Under the surface to hide inside the code.
Revealed, it says, “Pause, reflect, begin a new.”

palette

To choose a color

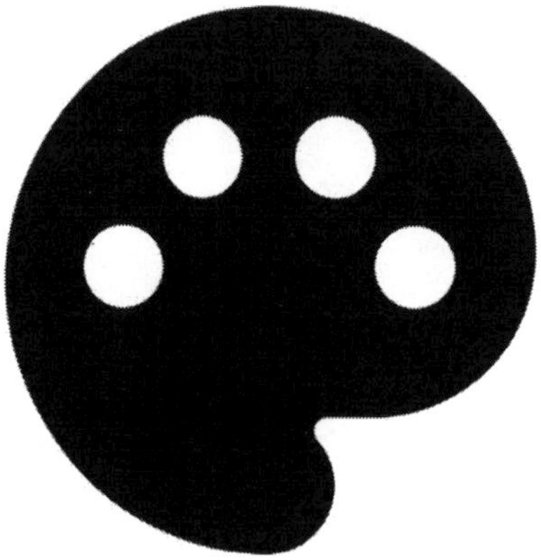

Black is not a color,
Monet liked to say,
Smearing his oils
To make a sky, a leaf, or wave--
Today we have more hues
Than eye can recognize,
But this icon still speaks of paint itself,
Fingers, and the act.

layers_clear

To remove all content from selected levels of an image

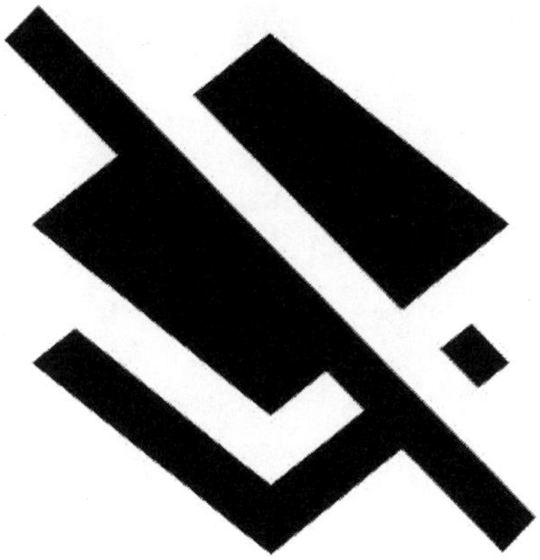

Beautiful ambiguity–
I see two layers devastated
By the slash. Are they broken
Into pieces,
Deleted,
Or just wiped clean?
Uncertain, I hesitate to tap.

flip_to_back

To switch foreground
for background

No somersaults here, just
One image wrestled underneath,
Squirming behind, within, obscured,
Or broken by what's on top--
A promised miracle of code,
Impossible in ink.

3D_rotation

To show an object from any angle

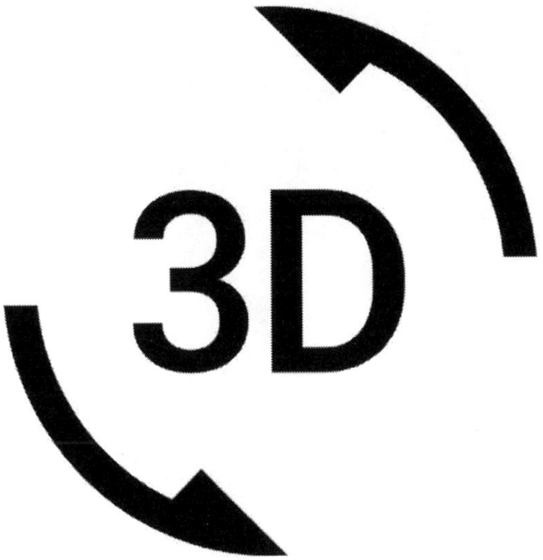

Revolve, reflect, explore,
Turn reality around, label
Depth as a dimension
And make insight
Depend upon
An unending dance.

bluetooth

To connect devices

Angular and sharp, like a letter chiselled
Into stone, this rune carries its own history,
Sending packets hopping along so many frequencies
That Harald Bluetooth, Viking king,
Might not recognize how his own sign
Has been redoubled, standardized, and spread
Like messages and music,
Point to point, near, and in our very air.

import-export

To bring in content, or send it out

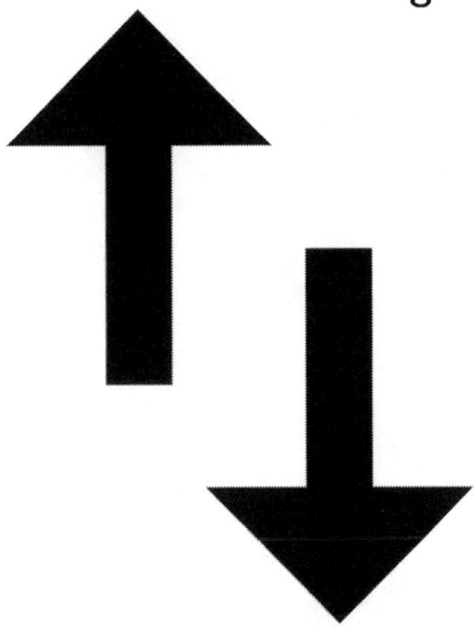

The mind imagines there's an up and a down,
It cannot see the mesh, the myriad
Handshakes, pings, check bits, and protocols
That traffic a thousand bits into one file sent
From a here to a there.
The icon's a mirage.

help

To get definitions, steps,
reference, or tips

Step by step to hell, we may elaborate
What you do not want to know, and omit
The concept, the map, the secret that
We guard, like truth, behind a maze
Of jargon, blind links, chaos, and contempt.
Now what was your question?

hash

To state the theme, or meme,
of a post

Does this look like hash to you?
Cross-hatching, yes, eight empty boxes
Surrounding a treasure, perhaps, but how
Did this mark come to mean number, pound,
Tag, space, and commentary? Add one phrase,
And it brings a stream of posts,
Imprisoning our attention in its grid.

download

To bring content or code
from the cloud

This icon lets us believe that data flows downhill,
As if a server farm could be a cloud, ready to burst.
Where now are the thousand-and-one exchanges
Swarming back-and-forth and all around–
Too complex, and alive.
Imagining that one click can strike lightening,
The mind prefers a simple summary.

calendar

To see or edit your appointments

When did we put our days into a grid,
And how did Today become a square?
This dark frame
Puts free time in a cell.

add_link

To take people to another site

In 1985 when Bill Atkinson came up with HyperCard
We had no metaphor for "click and go"--
Analogies with pipes and cables, synapses
And nets, even spiderwebs, tried to express
The leap we could make, the jump of faith.
This icon, like a USB port, makes the miracle routine.

bug_report

To submit a problem to be fixed

Click to add a bug.
Oh wait, it's a report.
The difference between the sign
And the significance
Makes me want to squash the form.

hide_source

To keep a competitor from
reading your original code

You cannot hide your source code from us.
Yes, you can disable keys that let us hackers
Scrape your secrets, you can obfuscate,
Encrypt, and comment out the guts.
But even dumb persistence can transform
Your gibberish and unhex your curse.

pinch

To zoom in

Ouch! It says to pinch, but shows a tap
And slide. Does this expand or shrink?
This icon counts on text
To say what imagery denies.

time_lapse

To make a slow activity
seem fast

Click here, the icon says,
To eat the impatient hour,
Accelerate the flow,
And make time itself collapse.
Appalled, my mind imagines
A tsunami of sunsets
Rushing into midnight.

route

To show a path from
here to there

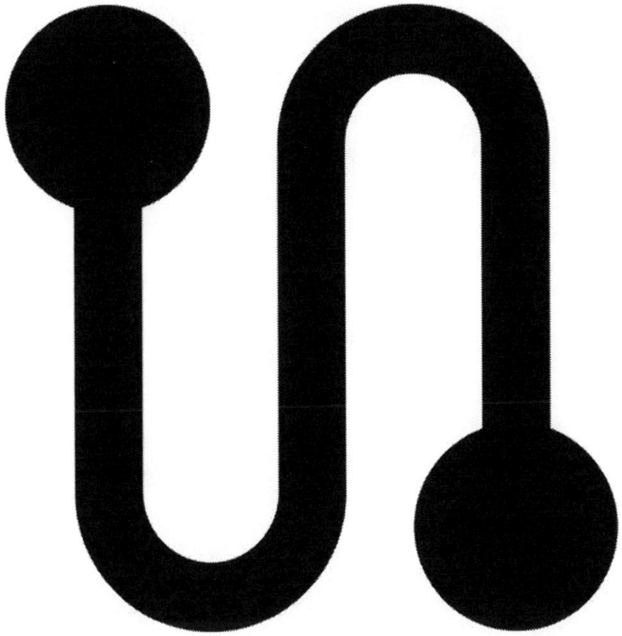

Is this the most direct?
From blob to blob, who chooses
To make U-turns? Perhaps
The icon means Meander.

portrait

To make a picture that is taller than wide

This icon is not exact.
It's square, but when it's tapped,
The frame gets tall and thin--
That aspect ratio
Blesses any vertical
And magnifies the head.

lens_blur

To make background objects
seem far off

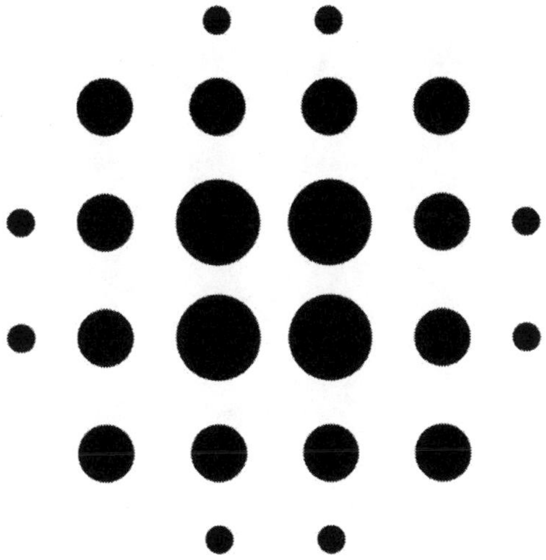

Why choose uncertainty, and interfere
With what we see, smearing Vaseline across
Our retina, turning Kodak clarity to mist?
Not Yayoi Kusama or Larry Poons,
But fake Monets, I think--
Nostalgia for depth.

crop

To cut out part of a picture

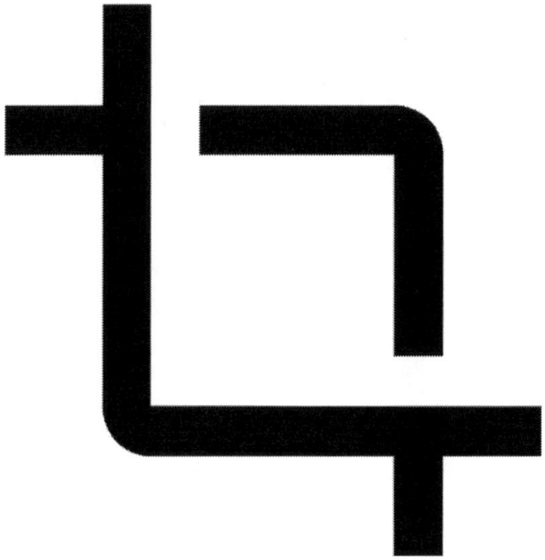

What gets cut? What survives?
This tangle's overthought,
Designed by a committee.
What harvest comes
When icons try, but fail
To say what they allow?

aspect_ratio

To adjust a picture to fit on your screen

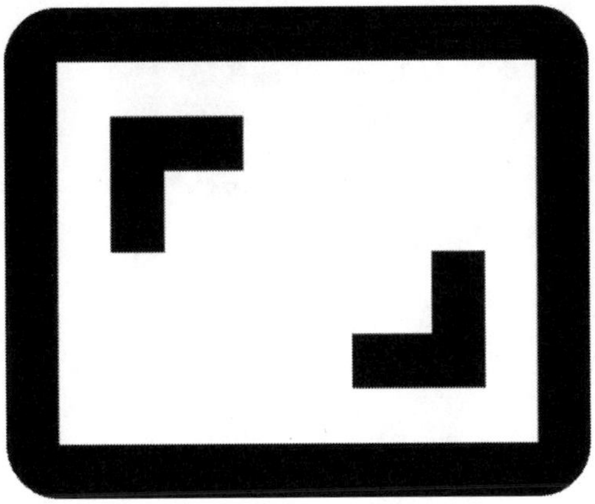

Squeezing or extruding,
You force the moving images
Into an unnatural frame.
You cut off context. You smear detail.
This is not second sight.
It's a fraction of the whole,
Yielding an irrational result.

zoom_in

To enlarge an image

When the image fails,
We turn to hover text. Here,
You show three metaphors at once.
Do you mean add, o
Or search,
Or magnify?
Significance dies, buried beneath
Too many meanings, too little thought.

traffic

To show how busy
the roads are

A primitive altar, perhaps,
Or a four-way stop,
Its label seems to promise flow,
But the picture says
"Go slow."

ice_cream

To bring up info about
an ice cream store

A magic landmark, a pin on the map,
The Cowlick, perhaps, in Daytona,
Mecca for the moo, coconut with cream,
It asks, what flavor would you like?
Just click and it arrives!

troubleshoot

To get help analyzing a problem

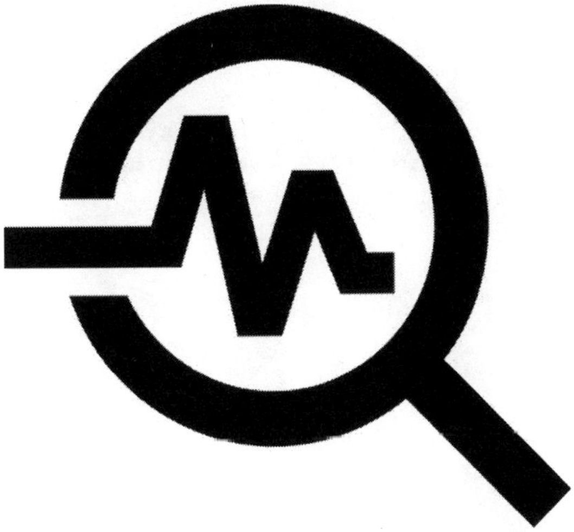

Don't give me lame workarounds,
Or force me to ask a group chat.
Admitting a problem is **not** enough.
Fix it!
With 5k known bugs, trouble always
Crawls inside your interface.

lock

To prevent changes

My ego says, "This is mine. You
Cannot break in, revise, or change--
I'm separate, unique, and pure.”
But spirit slips past the hardened steel,
And mind itself forgets the code.

`add_task`

To expand your guilt

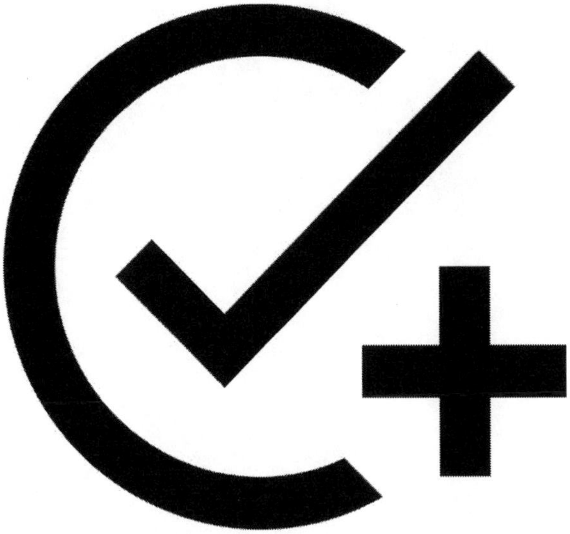

Who wants to add another task to
The endless circle of to-do and not yet
Done, checked off, delivered, and soon forgot?
Ambition is no plus,
And, hey, inertia's not a sin.

alarm_add

To set another time for it to go off

Behind the icon, what anxiety
Expands, what distress
Makes foreboding into warning,
Enlarging secret dread?
Will clamor, rattle, and ring
Bring true awakening?

bell

To display alerts or notifications

How heavy the brass dinner bell that called
My grandfather in from loading hay,
How delicate the little bell inside the phone
When its namesake, Alexander Graham, called.
But this icon, tiny, weightless,
Vibrates with unceasing alerts--
An attention parasite.

announcement

To call attention to news

Like a comment rising to a shout,
This icon introduces news with a whoop,
Posts notices with a hoot, and releases ordinary
Information as if it were an emergency alert.
Is the exclamation, then, the point?

assignment_add

To assign more homework

Oh no! More work!
Pile essay upon test,
Make dictée and précis
Recalculate the experiment
And, quick, slave, submit!

bookmark_added

To confirm you've set up
a shortcut to a web page

No book, no mark,
Just the idea, the original
Metaphor abandoned, leaving
An empty hieroglyph.
Hover text cannot overcome
A sign that checks itself.

question

To get an answer

?

Doubt rises in the cloud of unknowing,
Anger seizes me, anxiety stops my brain.
Why would I want to add another question?
And how could I perceive the truth
When you leave out steps, and multiply
Abstraction, jargon, and contempt?
This icon admits that its interface sucks.

information

To get a definition, procedure,
tip, or excuse

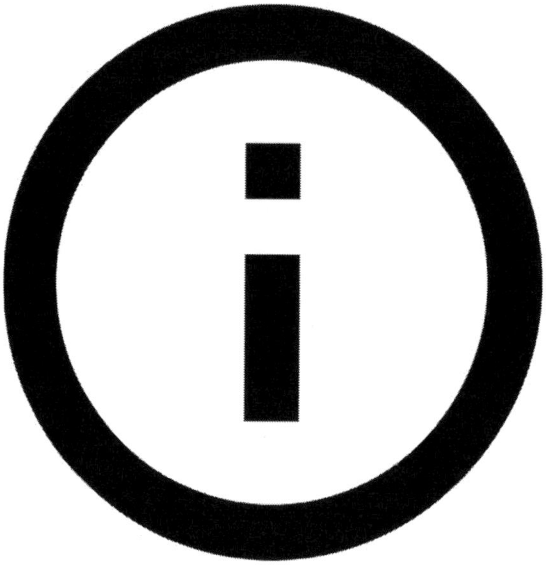

Caught in the perfect circle, the answer
Claims, modestly, “I can tell you how. I can
Define, explain, label, or give you a tip. In fact
I am so innocuous I lowercase my own identity,
Hypnotizing you with my one eye.”

lock_open

A signal that the file is open to changes

Not safe, but free, the file is open to
Updates or deletes, and the screen
Lets us in, defying security.
This icon confirms a state.
It does not save or guarantee
Anything other than availability.

insert_link

To let users jump to another location

Connect now, and extend the chain,
Tie one hot spot to a thousand, and make mind
Flow freely into this live wire, and
As your electrons surge through the mesh of nets,
Add your thread to the collective weave.

extension

To plug in or add
a function to a program

Oil slick or puzzle piece
It infiltrates and spreads,
A nubby parasite
Devouring but enlarging
The data and its host.

api

To let one Application talk to another
(via a Programming Interface)

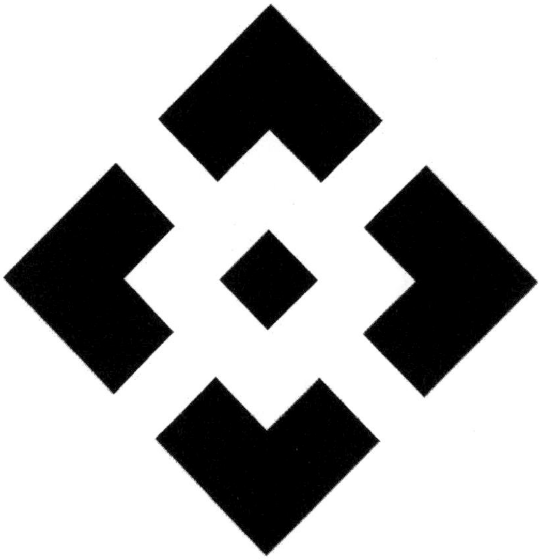

Is this an apiary where bees
Swarm, and share their tiny handshakes?
Does this promise a hive where honey
Forms in the interstices of the frame?
Or is it just 3.1415926535 extended to infinity?

wind

To display wind speeds

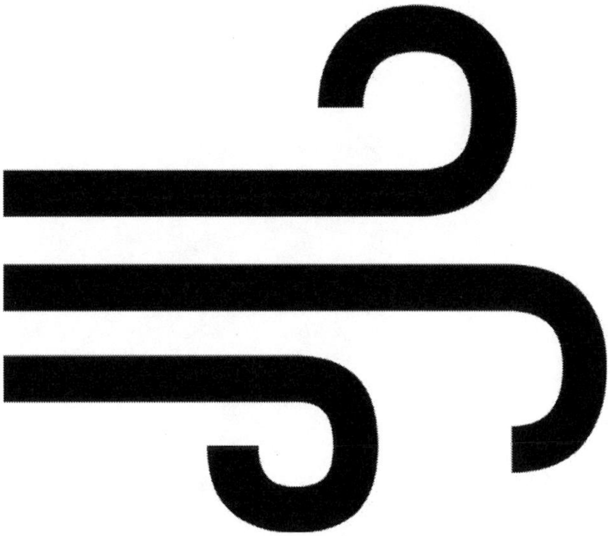

Click to see a thousand arrows flow
Swarming, turning as a school, pouring
Across the satellite map, like minnows in
The shallows, fleeing the cold, following
Warmth into cloud roads, mist, and swirl us
Out of our doldrums into sheer atmosphere.

fingerprint

To accept your swipe identifying
who you are

Maze or labyrinth,
Do the lines reveal
Who dares open or intrude?
Or does this smear, preserved, prove guilt?

ring_volume

To set the decibel level of the alert when you receive a call

Sound explodes from a handset like we've seen
In movies from the last century, one end
For talking, the other for listening, both tremulous
With what Ma Bell used to call a ring, now fractured
Into a hundred snippets of reconstituted melody.

outlet

To automate control over a device using this plug

So sad, this unhappy plug, letting
Electricity leak into the room, or spark from
Prong and ground, alternating on then off,
Live then dead, the uncertainty circling as it
Chooses to light up, shriek, or electrocute.

all_out

To send all output through a channel

altogether complete
entirely fully perfect
surrounding the whole

emptied and cleared
sent out and removed,
zero defies its square

percent

To express a number as
a fraction of 100

%

How mysterious the slash--
Is that two eyes and a nose, sniffing
Return on investment or your test score?
Or does the glyph divide zero by zero,
To yield infinity?

settings

To adjust what your device does, and how

This gear drives a thousand smaller ones, whirling
Inside an infinite hierarchy of tweaks that
Ripple unexpected consequences.
Will one change tip the sand pile,
And freeze the screen?
Fear vies with my desire for mastery.
Chance, not knowledge, spins this dial.

at

To show where we can reach you

@

Five to a dollar, one at 20 cents,
The word ***a*** worms its way
Around and in, and becomes a sign--
It ties a name to an address,
And, pigtail, maze, or escargot.
Its shape loops our identity.

file

To store information as a unit
that you can create, read, edit,
save, or delete.

How did a single piece of paper
With the corner bent down
Come to stand for an entire document,
One that's stored in assorted bits scattered
Around random memory?
Even a file is an imaginary being.

keyboard

To enter information
by typing

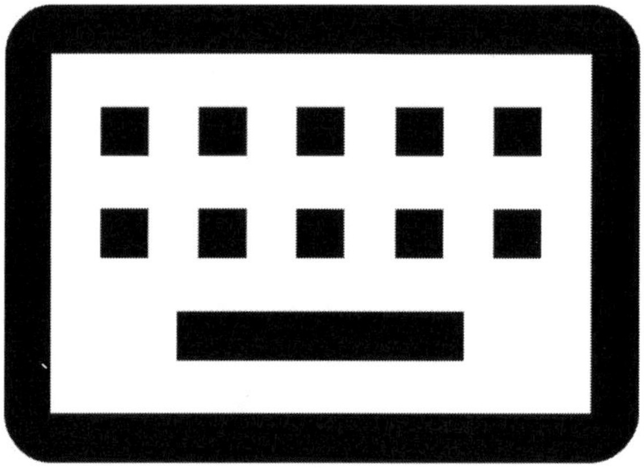

How did the alphabet get put into a grid?
All hail the typewriter and the linotype machine,
Engines faster than any pen, brush, or telegraph,
Slowed down by QWERTY, the illogical display.
So now speech acts as input, and the keys, rattling
Like ghosts, just remind us of learning to write
One letter at a time, spelling out our names.

menu

To display a list of
commands or options

When we were first creating
A user interface, we came up with lists:
But what genius decided to call them menus?
Where's the pie?
And how did these three lines
Become the symbol of so many options
To explore, dig down, and browse?

reply_all

*To send a response to everyone
who received an email*

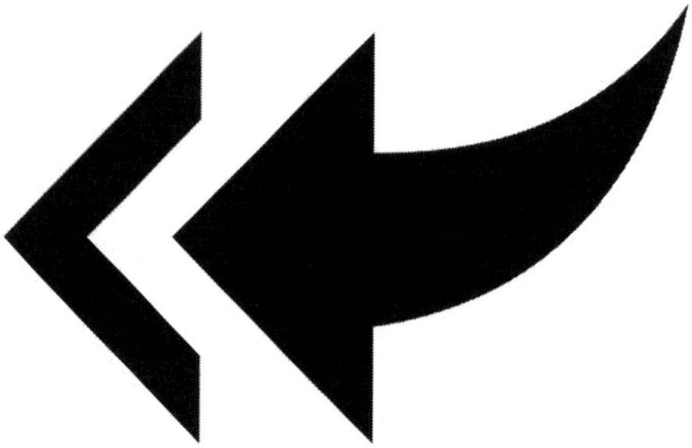

The most dangerous icon of all,
It distributes your sext, your confessional,
Your rant, your casual betrayal
To everyone, without recall.
And when you get the first odd replies,
Shame sends you racing back,
As you replay that one unthinking click.

ampersand

*To stand for **and***

&

Elegant emblem
Ornate placeholder
Connective pointer
Without alphabet or syllable
You represent and

The Set

Alphabetically by name

Other Books by Jonathan Reeve Price

Viewing Hokusai Viewing Mount Fuji, Communication Circle, 2020.

The Liquid Border: The Rio Grande from El Paso to the Gulf of Mexico, Communication Circle, 2020.

Write a Use Case: Gathering Requirements that Users can Understand, Communication Circle, 2020.

American Scenery: Thomas Cole vs NASA, Communication Circle, 2019.

Remapping Paris, A MuseumZero Exhibition, Communication Circle, 2018.

Get Past the Tags: How to Write (and Read) XML, Communication Circle, 2018.

Hot Text—Web Writing that Works! With Lisa Price, Peachpit Pearson, 2002.

Digital Imaging: The Official HP Guide, with Lisa Price, IDG Books, 1999.

Outlining Goes Electronic: A Study of the Impact of Media on our Understanding of the Role of Outlining in Virtual and Collaborative Conversations. ATTW Series, Ablex, 1999.

The Virtual Playhouse for the Macintosh, Hayden Books, 1994.

How to Communicate Technical Information, with Henry Korman, Adam Rochmes, Linda Urban, and Mick Renner. Benjamin/Cummings. 1993.

Classic Scenes. New American Library, 1979.

The Best Thing on TV: Commercials. Viking Press, Penguin Books, 1978.

Video Visions: A Medium Discovers Itself. New American Library, 1977.

Life Show: How to See Theater in Life and Life in Theater, with John Lahr. Viking

Press and Penguin Books. 1973. Reissued by Limelight Editions, 1990.

On Finnegans Wake (pamphlet). Grove Press. 1972.

Critics on Robert Lowell (editor). University of Miami Press, U.K. edition: Allen and Unwin. 1972.

To learn more...

Blog: http://museumzero.blogspot.com/

Linked In: http://www.linkedin.com/in/JonathanReevePrice

Amazon Author Page: https://www.amazon.com/author/jonathanprice

Web site: MuseumZero.Art

LAROUSSE
LES 1001 EXPRESSIONS
501 FRENCH VERBS
Visual Thinking
MANET

Made in United States
Troutdale, OR
11/03/2026

56852551R00071